Bug Boy
Beetle
Cookies
Written by Jeanne Willis
Illustrated by Ben Mantle

Dan did not have a dog or a cat.

He had lots of pet bugs!

Dan had **big bugs** and little bugs.
He had bugs in his room.

He had bugs in the garden.
BUG BOOK

Dan looked at a **big** bug.

He looked in his bug book.
It was a beetle!

Mum looked at the beetle.

"Can I have a tin to put him in?" said Dan.

"Put him in this cookie tin,"
said Mum.
"Thank you," said Dan.

Emma looked at the tin.
"Cookies!" said Emma.

"No," said Dan.
"There are no cookies in this tin!"

But Emma took the lid off the tin.

"Yuck, a bug!" said Emma.
She ran off.

"He is not a cookie
but he **is** sweet," said Dan.